kay and norma
dedicate this book
to all the children
who enjoy our stories

CLINKER MEETS THE FLYING SQUIRREL

By
KAY WITSCHEN

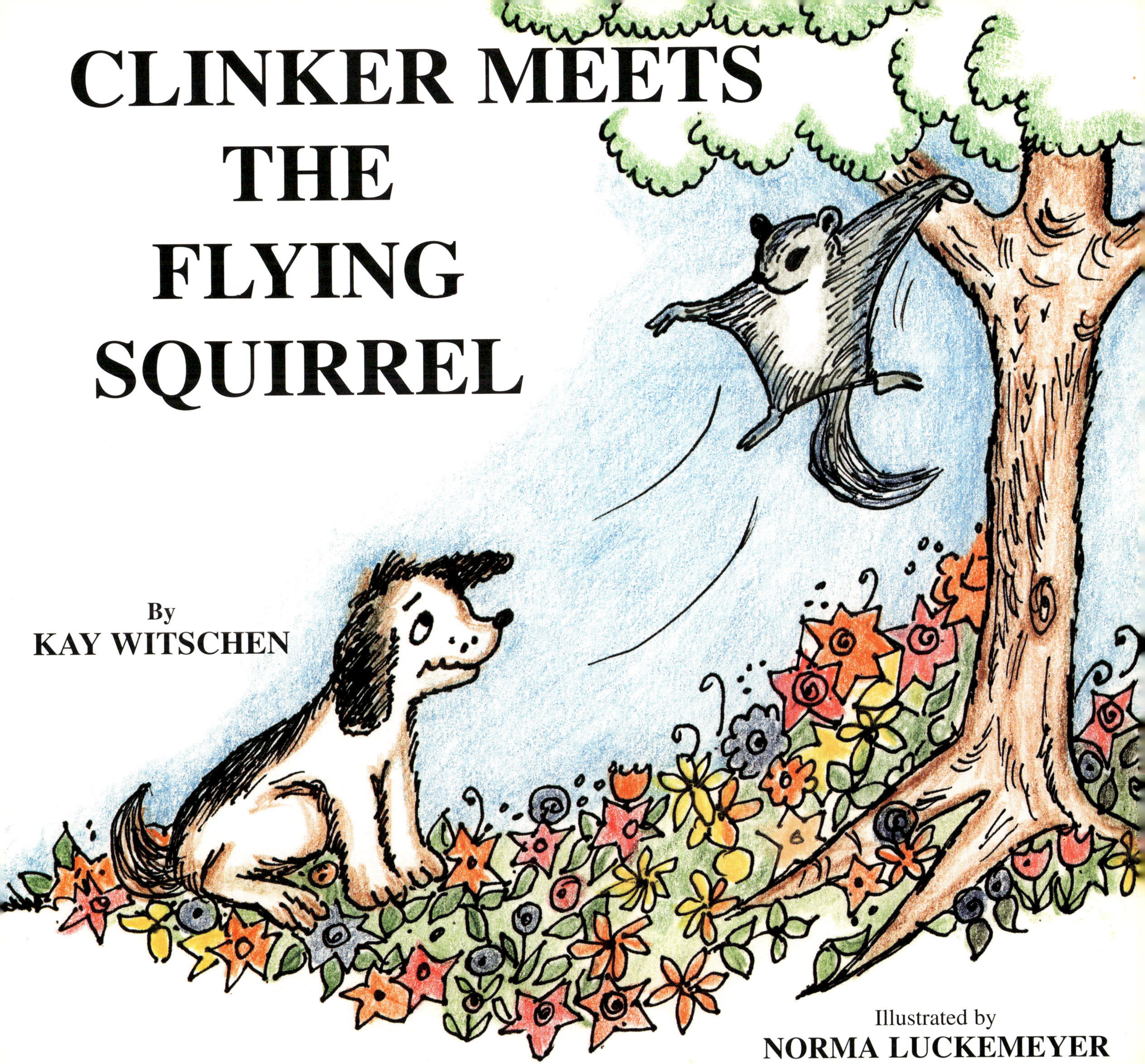

Illustrated by
NORMA LUCKEMEYER

CLINKER MEETS THE FLYING SQUIRREL

Clinker was walking in the woods on a perfect Spring day. He felt like the luckiest dog in the world - no flea to bother him and no kitten causing him problems. He looked around at all the beautiful trees.

There it was! The perfect spot to take a little rest.

He snuggled down on a cozy bed of leaves under a big oak tree. He had just dozed off when he was awakened by a strange sound.

"Hey you - dog
Get away from this tree
You can't sleep here
It belongs to me."

"Who are you?" Clinker asked.

"And WHERE are you?"

he said as he looked first to the right - then to the left -

trying to spot the intruder.

"I'm right here
Above your head
Now go elsewhere
To make your bed."

Clinker looked up and on a branch high in the tree he saw a very strange animal.

"Well I see WHERE YOU ARE

BUT

WHAT

ARE

YOU?"

"You foolish dog
I'm a flying squirrel
It's none of your business
But my name is Earl."

"Oh, that's very funny," answered Clinker. "Everyone knows squirrels do not fly. Now be quiet and do not BOTHER me. I'm going back to sleep."

Clinker was just falling asleep again when all of a sudden

POP! WHIZ!

BANG!

SMACK! POW!

something was hitting him.

ACORNS!

That ANIMAL was throwing ACORNS at him.

"Why are you being so mean?
I didn't do anything to you. You stop that right now - you THING.
I will not be chased away from this tree.
This woods and THIS TREE belong to everyone."

"That's what you think
But know one thing
That in this tree
I am the KING."

"O.K. That's it King-Big-Shot-Earl. I give up. Show me you can fly and I'll leave." said Clinker.

Earl leaped from the tree, spread his very strange wings and glided down towards Clinker. He was so angry he did not watch where he was going and

THUD!

BANG!

he flew straight into a big tree trunk.

Earl

was

not

moving!

Clinker sat still for a moment, and watched and waited, not knowing what to expect. Should he do something? He hoped the squirrel was not dead. No - he could see that Earl was still breathing. He would probably wake up any minute.

Suddenly a dark shadow passed overhead.

Clinker looked up and saw a

VERY

VERY

LARGE

HAWK

So large that it even frightened Clinker.

OH NO!! The hawk was making a dive toward the squirrel. Clinker sat by Earl and barked and barked. Every time the hawk got near, Clinker growled and showed his teeth, trying to look as scary as he could.

At last the hawk changed his mind about having the squirrel for dinner and soared upward toward the sky.

Clinker was so happy to see Earl starting to move. He sat quietly by until the squirrel was fully awake.

"I saw the hawk
And I want to say
You can sleep by my tree
Any old day."

"Yeah, well it was nothing," said a blushing Clinker. "And you sure CAN fly. Now you better fly back up where you are safe."

"When I go UP
I cannot fly
I must climb
To get up high."

"You better scoot on up the tree just in case that hawk comes back this way. I'll finish my nap under your tree, if you don't mind. By the way, my name is Clinker. Clinker the WALKING dog." (And, Clinker was thinking, sometimes Clinker the SCARED dog - especially when I see a swooping hawk.)

At last, Clinker thought, I can get that nap I've been waiting for. He was just drifting off to sleep when he heard:

"Clinker I'm very sorry
For being rude to you
But you are the only dog
That I ever knew."

"That's okay. Wait until I tell my friends I met you - EARL THE FLYING SQUIRREL - they probably -won't -believe -me..Z...Z...z...z..

THE END